HAPPY BIRTHDAY!

PHOTOS: Page 19 The Granger Collection; page 25 (all) The Bettmann Archive; page 27 D. Donne Bryant.

First Steck-Vaughn Edition 1992

Copyright © 1989 American Teacher Publications

Published by Steck-Vaughn Company

Library of Congress number: 89-3866

Library of Congress Cataloging in Publication Data.

Motomora, Mitchell.
  Happy birthday!/Mitchell Motomora; illustrated by Mary Young Duarte.

  (Real readers)
  Summary: Describes birthday customs and their origins, including lighting candles, sending cards, and playing games such as the breaking of a piñata.
  1. Birthdays—Juvenile literature. [1. Birthdays.] I. Duarte, Mary Young, ill. II. Title. III. Series.
GT2430.M68   1989   394.Z—dc19   89-3866

ISBN 0-8172-3510-8   hardcover library binding

ISBN 0-8114-6706-6   softcover binding

      5 6 7 8 9 0   96 95 94 93

HAPPY BIRTHDAY!

by
Mitchell Motomora
illustrated by
Mary Young Duarte

RSVP
RAINTREE STECK-VAUGHN
P U B L I S H E R S
The Steck-Vaughn Company

Austin, Texas

What will you do on your birthday? Will you have a cake with candles on top? Will you have a party where you play games? Will you get birthday cards and gifts? Will people sing "Happy Birthday to You"?

There are lots of things you can do to have fun on your birthday.

Today is Jill's birthday. This is what Jill does. She has cup cakes for all the boys and girls. She has a cup cake for Ms. Drake, too.

Ms. Drake made a hat for Jill and a birthday card, too. Jill puts the hat on. Ms. Drake puts a candle in Jill's cup cake. All the boys and girls sing "Happy Birthday to You."

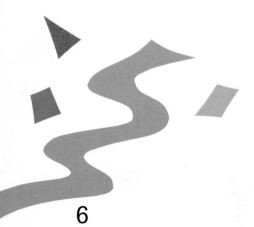

Today is Ben's birthday. This is what Ben does. Ben is at home with Mom and Dad. Ben does not have a big party this year. But Ben does get a big birthday gift! Mom and Dad have a bike for Ben!

Today is Ellen's birthday. This is what Ellen does. Ellen will have 2 parties, 1 with Mom and 1 with Dad.

Ellen has a party at home with Mom. Boys and girls come to the party and play games. Aunt May and Uncle Bob come, too.

Ellen will have a party at Dad's, too. Dad has made Ellen a cake. Grandma and Grandpa come. They all sing "Happy Birthday to You."

Today is Shawn's birthday. It is
Thomas's birthday, too. This is what
Shawn and Thomas do. They have 1 big
party. But they have 2 cakes!

Today is Rita's birthday. This is what Rita does. Rita has a big party. All the boys and girls play the Breaking the Piñata game.

The pinata is filled with good things. The boys and girls hit the pinata. Pop! Out come all the treats!

You can see that there are lots of things that you can do on your birthday. Candles and a cake, singing "Happy Birthday to You," birthday cards, and parties with games like Breaking the Piñata are all birthday customs. Customs are things that people have done for years and years.

Why do people put candles on a birthday cake?

This custom started about 200 years ago in Germany. People in Germany made good candles. They started to make little candles to put on birthday cakes. They said that it means good luck to blow out all the candles in 1 blow!

Today, boys and girls in lots of places
blow out candles on birthday cakes.
PUFF! They want to blow out the
candles with 1 blow!

Why do we sing "Happy Birthday to You"?

This custom comes from America. About 100 years ago, Mildred Hill and Patty Hill made this up. "Happy Birthday to You" made a big hit!

Today, people in lots of places sing "Happy Birthday to You."

Why do we have birthday cards?

This custom comes from England. About 100 years ago, people in England started to make birthday cards. People in Canada and America started to make birthday cards, too.

Today, people in lots of places get lots and lots of birthday cards.

Why do we have parties with games like Breaking the Piñata?

Breaking the Piñata is a game that comes from Mexico. This custom started about 300 years ago. If you break the piñata, good things come out. It is good luck to break the piñata.

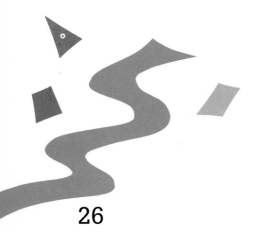

Today, boys and girls in lots of places play Breaking the Piñata. They play games like Pin the Tail on the Donkey, too. Playing games at a birthday party is fun.

Your birthday is your day. You may have a cake with candles. You may have a party with games. You may get birthday cards and gifts. Your birthday is your day to feel good and have fun.

What will you do on your birthday?

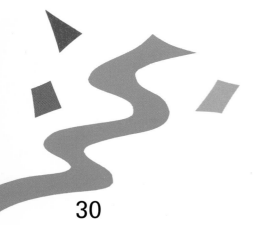

Sharing the Joy of Reading

Beginning readers enjoy reading books on their own. Reading a book is a worthwhile activity in and of itself for a young reader. However, a child's reading can be even more rewarding if it is shared. This sharing can enhance your child's appreciation — both of the book and of his or her own abilities.

   Now that your child has read **Happy Birthday!**, you can help extend your child's reading experience by encouraging him or her to:

- Retell the story or key concepts presented in this story in his or her own words. The retelling can be oral or written.

- Create a picture of a favorite character, event, or concept from this book.

- Express his or her own ideas and feelings about the subject of this book and other things he or she might want to know about this subject.

Here is an activity that you can do together to help extend your child's appreciation of this book: Help your child make a birthday card for a family member, friend, or teacher. Supply paper, crayons or markers, paste, glitter, and other materials. Encourage your child to decorate the card with pictures showing various birthday customs. Make sure to have the child give or send the card in time for the recipient's birthday.